Dance

of the

Dolphins

To Winton Fletcher,
   I love that you chose my dolphin
book, Winton. Dolphins are a huge
part of keeping our ocean's clean. Perhaps
you and I can be good stewards for
dolphins together!
                              XOXO,
                              Pat Gleichauf

By Patricia Gleichauf

Illustrated by Karen Staszko

PAGE PUBLISHING, INC.
Conneaut Lake, PA

First originally published by Page Publishing 2021

ISBN 978-1-6624-4989-5 (pbk)
ISBN 978-1-6624-4991-8 (hc)
ISBN 978-1-6624-4990-1 (digital)

Printed in the United States of America

To Caroline and Kevin, who took all of the lessons we taught them and made us proud. xoxo

All people in the world belong to a group called humans. Every.single.one.

All porpoises, dolphins, and whales belong to a group called cetaceans. BARRING. NONE.

Humans and cetaceans are mammals. They live on land and in water near and far. Mammals are warm-blooded. Their body temperature stays much the same no matter where they are.

Most mammals have hair that helps keep them warm whenever cold air creeps in.

Cetaceans have a fat layer that holds in their warmth from the tip of their beak to their tail fin.

Sometimes dolphins look like sharks. But dolphins are mammals and sharks are fish. They can easily be identified.

Dolphin tails are horizontal. They move up and down.
Fish tails are vertical and move side to side.

Like all mammals, dolphins breathe air into their lungs. They swim underwater then launch into the air for a breath.

They breathe through a blowhole on the top of their heads before diving once more to an amazing depth.

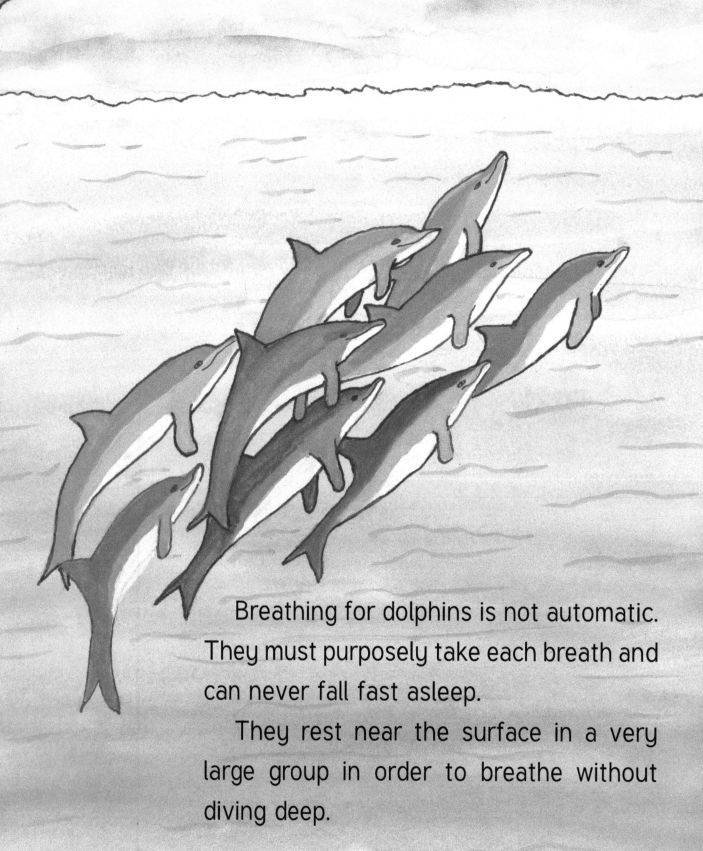

Breathing for dolphins is not automatic. They must purposely take each breath and can never fall fast asleep.

They rest near the surface in a very large group in order to breathe without diving deep.

It is called logging when dolphins rest in a group. They lie flat in a row with a purpose. If one falls asleep, forgetting to breathe, another nudges it up to the surface.

Dolphin babies are called calves and are born underwater. Like people, they are born alive.

Mama guides her calf up to take a first breath in order for it to survive.

An "auntie" dolphin swims nearby when a calf is born.
She stays close to assist if there is a need.

Calves swim close to their mother's side, using her slipstream to keep up their speed.

Baby dolphins are nourished with milk that they receive from their mother.

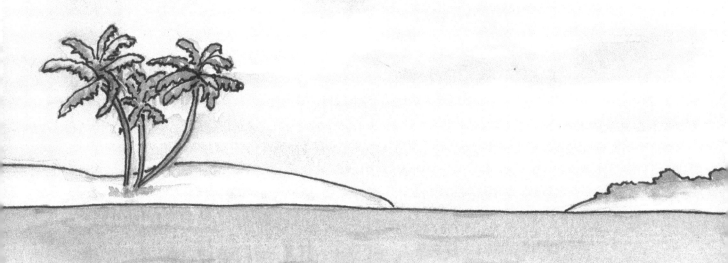

It helps grow the layer that keeps them warm. This layer of fat is called blubber.

Dolphins love jumping and twisting and chasing each other. They move together as if in a dance.

They cluster together when worried or scared, uniting to show a strong stance.

Dolphins often travel in groups called pods. Staying together helps them protect their young.

Their eyes can each move in a different direction to see danger before it has sprung.

Dolphins have exceptional hearing. They sense the direction of sound underwater and can tell when they are being pursued.

They create a picture from the sounds they are hearing. This is helpful when searching for food.

Nearly all dolphins live in salt water. Best known are the common and bottlenose dolphins. These are playful, friendly, and smart.

They will swim beside boats for hours, gracefully dancing until they must part.

A few types of dolphins live in the freshwater rivers of Asia and South America. River dolphins are very different than ocean dolphins. Their hearing is good, but their vision is dim. They rarely jump and slowly swim.

Porpoises are a smaller type of saltwater dolphin. Like their larger dolphin cousins, they eat crustaceans, squid, and fish.

While larger dolphins are social and friendly, porpoises are bashful and skittish.

Dolphins eat older and sickly sea creatures. For dolphins this is routine. They stop disease from spreading, which helps keep our oceans healthy and clean.

When dolphins dance in our oceans, they play an essential role. We should all do our best to protect them. It is a very important goal.

AWARDS AND RECOGNITION

Horses of the Sea, 2018
Gold Medal from Florida Authors
& Publishers Association

Starfish Gazing, 2019
2nd Place in the Purple Dragonfly
Children's Book Competition

Sea Turtles Circle, 2020
5-Star Readers' Favorite Review
Eric Hoffer Book Award Finalist
International Children's Book Competition Finalist
Readers' Favorite Non-Fiction
Children's Book Awards Finalist
Purple Dragonfly Children's Book Competition:
2nd Place, Age 5 & Up
Honorable Mention, Age 5 & Under

Coral Gardens, 2021
Nonfiction Author's Association Gold Medal
Eric Hoffer Grand Prize Finalist
DaVinci Eye Finalist for Cover Design

Honorable Mention Children's Category
International Book Award Finalist in Children's
Picture Book, Hardcover Nonfiction
5-Star Readers' Favorite Review
Purple Dragonfly Children's Book Competition:
1st Place, Children's Nonfiction
2nd Place, Best Illustrations
Honorable Mention, Picture Books Age 6 & Older

Under the Sea Series, 2019
Moonbeam Children's Book Awards Bronze Medal

About the Author

Pat Gleichauf lives in Upstate New York with her husband, Jack. Writing for children is her dream come true. She is dedicated to children's literacy, and her goal is to "hook kids on books." Pat does not miss an opportunity to read her books to students at schools and libraries. She uses this time to encourage children to follow their dreams.

About the Illustrator

Karen Staszko has been creating beautiful watercolor paintings for the past thirty years. She studied watercolor painting for seventeen years and has been teaching it for eleven years. Karen and her husband, Meron, are now living in North Ridgeville, Ohio, to be closer to their daughter and grandson. They lived for eleven years in Southwest Florida. Karen loves art in any form. Her passion is teaching art.